Chicks Hatching

This is a hen.

eye —

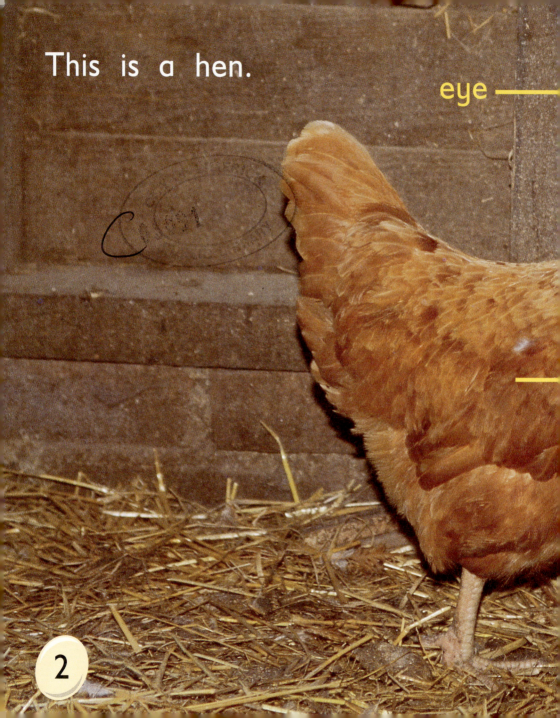

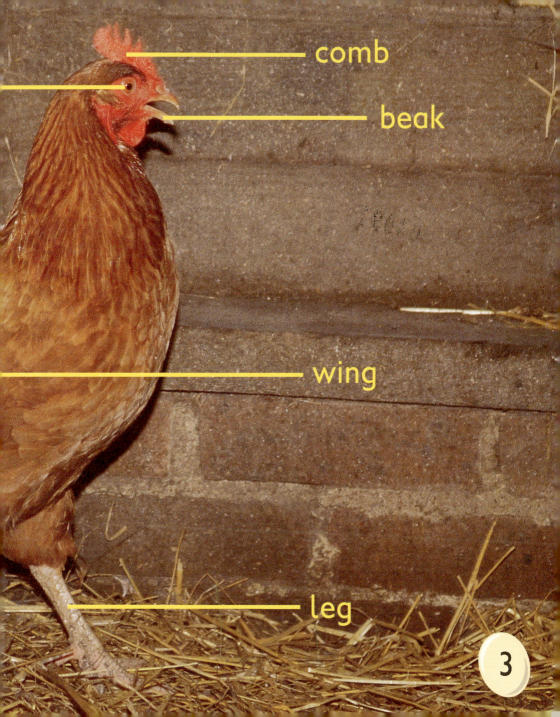

comb

beak

wing

leg

3

This is her nest.

The hen lays four eggs.

Day 1

It is small...

Day 7

it grows bigger...

It is time
for the chick to hatch.

Here is the beak.

Here is the head.

Here is the chick.

13

The hen has four chicks.

15

Glossary

beak

chick

egg

head

hen

nest